Rosa Parks

FIGHT FOR FREEDOM

Rosa Parks

FIGHT FOR FREEDOM

by Keith Brandt
illustrated by Gershom Griffith

This edition published 1998 by Troll Communications L.L.C.

Printed in the United States of America.

10   9   8   7   6   5   4

Cover art by Shi Chen.

Library of Congress Cataloging-in-Publication Data

Brandt, Keith, (date)
    Rosa Parks: fight for freedom / by Keith Brandt; illustrated by
Gershom Griffith.
p.   cm.
    Summary: A biography of the woman whose action led to the
desegregation of buses in Montgomery, Alabama, in the 1950's and who
was an important figure in the early days of the civil rights movement.
    ISBN 0-8167-2831-3 (lib. bdg.)   ISBN 0-8167-4558-7 (pbk.)
    1. Parks, Rosa, 1913-   —Juvenile literature. 2. Afro-Americans—
Alabama—Montgomery—Biography—Juvenile literature. 3. Civil
rights workers—Alabama—Montgomery—Biography—Juvenile literature.
4. Montgomery (Ala.)—Biography—Juvenile literature. 5. Afro-Americans—
Civil rights—Alabama—Montgomery—Juvenile literature.
6. Segregation in transportation—Alabama—Montgomery—History—20th
century—Juvenile literature. 7. Montgomery (Ala.)—Race relations—
Juvenile literature.   [1. Parks, Rosa, 1913-   . 2. Afro-Americans—
Biography. 3. Afro-Americans—Civil rights.]
I. Griffith, Gershom, ill.   II. Title.
F334.M753P3825   1993
323'.092—dc20
    [B]   92-34939

Rosa Parks

FIGHT FOR FREEDOM

It was early in the evening of December 1, 1955. Rosa Parks finished work at the Montgomery Fair Department Store and caught a bus to go home. She was tired after a long day of sewing in the store's tailor shop.

Mrs. Parks paid her fare, found an empty seat, and sat down. The bus soon filled with passengers. The black people sat in the back and the white people sat in the front. In those days, black and white people were often separated that way in the American South. This separation is called racial segregation. It was the law, and in Montgomery, Alabama, this kind of law was strictly enforced.

Rosa Parks sat in the middle of the bus. It was all right for blacks to sit there if no white person had to stand. But on that evening, as the bus filled, a white man was left without a seat. The driver told Mrs. Parks and the three other black people in her row to get up and move to the back of the bus. The others followed his orders. Mrs. Parks stayed in her seat.

The driver stood and walked back to where Mrs. Parks was sitting. "Are you going to stand up?" he asked her.

"No," she said calmly.

"Well, I'm going to have you arrested," the driver said.

"You may do that," Rosa Parks answered.

The driver left the bus and called the police. Mrs. Parks didn't move. Two policemen arrived and asked her why she didn't stand. Mrs. Parks responded with a question of her own. "Why do you all push us around?" she asked.

One of the officers answered, "The law is the law and you're under arrest."

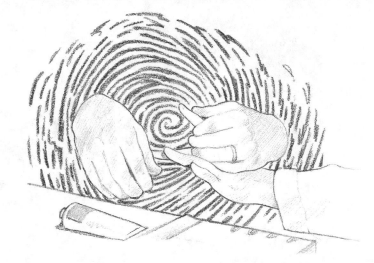

Mrs. Parks was taken to jail, where she was fingerprinted and put in a cell—all because she refused to give up her seat on a public bus.

Word of Mrs. Parks's arrest spread quickly. Three of her friends arrived at the jail to arrange for her release. They were Clifford and Virginia Durr, and Edgar D. Nixon. Mr. and Mrs. Durr were white. He was a lawyer, and they were both active members of the civil rights movement.

E.D. Nixon, a black man, was regional director of the Brotherhood of Sleeping Car Porters, the first black trade union in America. He was also president of the Alabama chapter of the National Association for the Advancement of Colored People (NAACP). Mrs. Parks was also a member of the NAACP, serving as secretary of the Montgomery, Alabama branch.

Mrs. Parks was allowed to leave with Nixon and the Durrs. Raymond Parks had also arrived by then, and he took his wife home. He was very relieved Mrs. Parks was safe. So was Mrs. Parks's mother, Leona McCauley. They knew it was dangerous for black people to go against white authority in the South. They both told Mrs. Parks to pay the fourteen-dollar fine and end the whole matter.

But it was just beginning. When Rosa Parks refused to give up her seat on the bus, she started another American revolution. Mrs. Parks decided to challenge the bus segregation law. She talked it over with Mr. Nixon and the Durrs, and they promised to join in the fight. That night they agreed on what steps to take.

The first big decision was to refuse to pay the fine. It meant that Mrs. Parks might have to go to jail. But she was ready for that.

The next step was to organize the whole black community to boycott the city's buses. (A boycott is when people join together and refuse to buy a product or use a service.) The city of Montgomery earned a large amount of money from bus fares. Most of those fares were paid by black people. The boycott's aim was to make the city lose money if they kept the bus segregation law.

Late on the night of December 1, a group called the Women's Political Council met. They printed a notice that was distributed to blacks all over the city. It read, "This woman's case will come up on Monday, December 5. We are, therefore, asking every Negro to stay off the buses Monday in protest of the arrest and trial. Don't ride the buses to work, to town, to school, or anywhere on Monday.... Please, children and grown-ups, don't ride the bus at all on Monday."

Word of the boycott spread during the weekend. Ministers of black churches used their Sunday sermons to talk about the boycott. They praised the courage of Rosa Parks. They told every churchgoer to pass the word to friends, relatives, and neighbors.

The boycott on Monday was a huge success. Hardly any black people took a bus that day. Empty bus followed empty bus all around the city. On that same Monday morning Rosa Parks appeared in court. She was found guilty of breaking the Montgomery segregation law. She refused to pay the fourteen-dollar fine. Instead, her lawyer filed an appeal. This meant that the case had to be heard by a higher court. Only the higher court could actually change the segregation law.

When Mrs. Parks and her lawyer left the courtroom they were stunned to see a crowd of about 500 black people standing silently on the sidewalk and the courthouse steps. When they saw Mrs. Parks, they greeted her with cheers and applause.

Mrs. Parks was thrilled. Tears came to her eyes. For the first time in her memory, the black community was openly united. At that moment, Rosa Parks knew she had done the right thing. She also knew there was a lot more that needed to be done.

That night there was a meeting at the Holt Street Baptist Church. The organizers weren't sure how many people would show up. They knew that the black citizens of Montgomery had walked miles that day to support the boycott, and everybody was exhausted. But that didn't stop them from coming.

Minute by minute, the church filled until there were no more seats. Hundreds gathered on the church grounds and in the streets surrounding the building. Loudspeakers had to be set up outside to carry the words of the meeting to everyone.

The big question to be decided at the meeting was, will the boycott continue? The black people were tired. Some were afraid. The white community was angry. Everyone knew what dangers lay ahead—loss of jobs, arrests, violence . . . maybe even death.

Then a new voice spoke up. It was the twenty-six-year-old minister from the Dexter Avenue Baptist Church. He had lived in Montgomery less than a year, and most of the people in the city did not know much about him. His name was the Reverend Martin Luther King, Jr.

King began by speaking about the history of segregation. "There comes a time that people get tired," he said. "We are here this evening to say . . . that we are tired . . . of being kicked about by the brutal feet of oppression."

He also spoke about the dangers of carrying on a boycott. Then King talked about the need for a boycott, and about the rightness of it, warning that there must be no violence on the part of the black community.

"The only weapon that we have in our hands this evening is the weapon of protest," he said, adding that this "just action" had to lead to freedom.

The crowd hung on the Reverend Martin Luther King's every word. When he finished speaking, there was a vote for continuing the boycott. Every man, woman, and child roared approval. The boycott went on!

Rosa Parks became a symbol because of her brave act. In that way she was special. But in other ways she was a typical black American. Her history is the story of many black people in the American South.

Rosa Parks's roots were in Africa. Her ancestors were brought to America by force, and put to work as slaves. Slavery ended after the Civil War, but life didn't become much easier for black people.

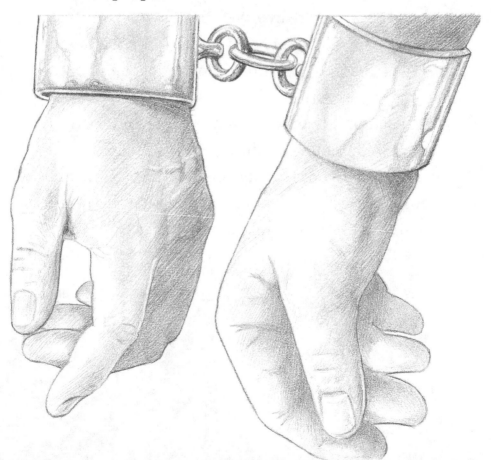

Rosa Parks was born on February 4, 1913, into a world of segregation and racism. At the time her family lived in Tuskegee, Alabama, where her father, James McCauley, worked as a carpenter. Soon after Rosa was born the McCauleys moved to nearby Abbeville, to live with James's family. A few years later Rosa's parents separated. Rosa did not see her father again until she was grown up.

Mrs. McCauley took Rosa and Rosa's baby brother Sylvester to live with her own parents, in Pine Level, Alabama. Then Mrs. McCauley, who was a teacher, went back to work to support herself and her children.

Today, a good teacher like Mrs. McCauley can get a job in any public school. But in those days, a black teacher could only teach black children in separate black schools. Black teachers were also paid much less than white teachers.

There was a great difference between education for blacks and whites. White schools were well-built, well-equipped, and the teachers were well-paid. White children had textbooks, heated classrooms, buses, and a full school year.

Black children went to run-down schools with no heat, no desks, no textbooks, and no school supplies. They had to walk to school, often many miles. And they went to school only part of every year. The rest of the time black children were expected to work in the fields, picking cotton, weeding, and doing other farm chores.

Although the system was cruel and unfair, black people had no way to change it. The laws made them second-class citizens and kept them that way. Black people who protested or behaved like free human beings were punished. Sometimes the punishment was the loss of a job or land. Often it was much worse.

All over the South there were gangs of white people who used violence and murder to control black people. The worst of these groups was the Ku Klux Klan (KKK). Klan members wore white sheets and hoods to hide their identities. They often committed their terrible deeds at night, burning churches and homes, and killing any blacks they found. They were never punished for any of their crimes.

When Mrs. McCauley went back to teaching, her parents, Rose and Sylvester Edwards, took care of the children. Mr. and Mrs. Edwards owned eighteen acres of land. They grew corn, fruit, yams, and many other vegetables. They raised their own pigs, cows, and chickens, and caught fish in a nearby creek. Though the family was poor, there was always enough to eat. Life on the farm for little Rosa and Sylvester was happy and secure. But there was always a cloud that hung over their lives. It was the ever-present danger of the KKK and other racist groups.

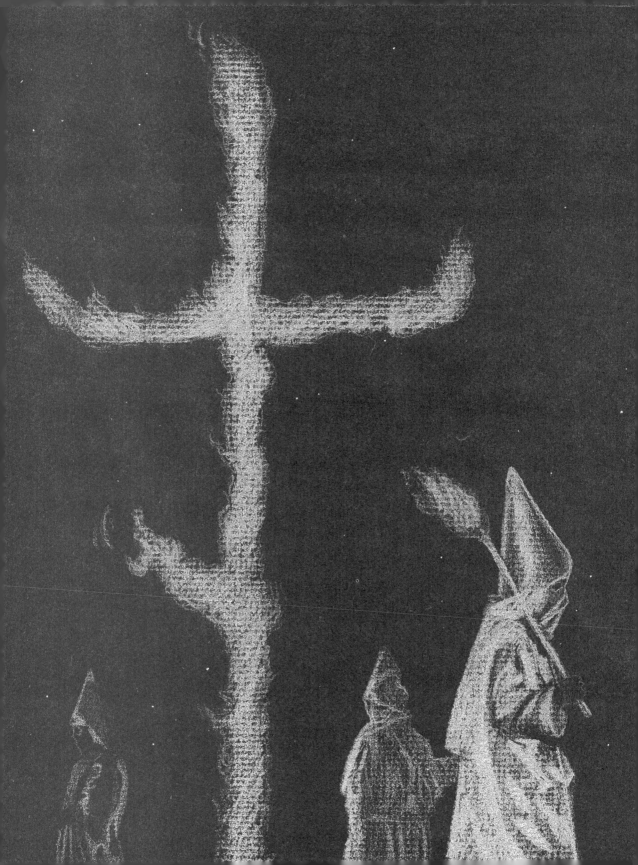

One of Rosa's first experiences with racism came when she was five years old. The KKK was very active in her part of Alabama. They rode around at night, destroying black churches, burning crosses on black property, breaking into black homes and killing the people who lived there. Every night, Mr. Edwards sat in his home with a shotgun close by. If the Klan attacked his house, he was ready for them.

"I don't know how long I would last if they came breaking in here," he told Rosa. "But I'm getting the first one who comes through the door."

On those nights Rosa sat on the floor next to her grandfather's rocking chair. He told her stories about his parents and about his mother's difficult life as a slave. He talked about the Civil War, and what happened when Yankee soldiers came and told the slaves they were free.

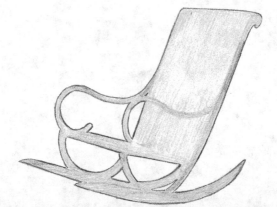

Rosa loved and admired Grandfather Edwards. He had a very hard life, but he did not let it defeat him. He had an inner strength that was unshakable, and he taught his family not to put up with bad treatment from anyone.

Grandfather Edwards spoke to black and white people with equal dignity and honesty. Everyone knew he expected the same respect from them. It was these qualities that Rosa took for her own. They gave her a solid core of values that stayed with her the rest of her life.

Mrs. McCauley's teaching job kept her away from home all week, but she always spent weekends with her children. During those weekends she taught Rosa and Sylvester to read and write. Even before Rosa started school, she had a strong love of books and learning.

The school Rosa attended had one room for all classes, from first through sixth grade. Sixth grade was the end of schooling for most black children in Alabama. In the entire state there were only a couple of black junior high and high schools, and they were in the big cities.

When Rosa finished sixth grade she wanted more education. Mrs. McCauley took her daughter to Montgomery. There, the eleven-year-old enrolled in the Montgomery Industrial School for Girls, better known as Miss White's school. Alice White, who founded the school, came from Massachusetts. She and all her teachers were white. All the students were black. It was the first time that Rosa was treated as an equal by white people.

Miss White's school was private. The state did not support it in any way. Families who could afford to pay for their daughters' education, did so. The rest of the money to run the school came from local churches and from Mr. Julius Rosenwald, a rich and generous man who believed in education for all people.

Mrs. McCauley paid for Rosa's first year at Miss White's school. After that, her daughter was awarded a full scholarship. Rosa studied the usual school subjects, including English, science, arithmetic, and geography. The girls also learned sewing, cooking, and some nursing.

After Rosa had finished eighth grade, the school closed. Miss White had grown too old to continue working. Rosa stayed in Montgomery and enrolled at Booker T. Washington Junior High School, where she completed the ninth grade. Then she enrolled at the Alabama State Teachers' College for Negroes. This college trained black teachers. The students learned by teaching at a high school run by the college. Rosa attended this high school for the tenth and part of the eleventh grade.

Then Grandmother Edwards got very sick and Rosa had to leave school to take care of her. After Rosa's grandmother died, the teenager returned to Montgomery and got a job in a shirt factory. This allowed Rosa to earn enough to live on while she went back to school. But then Mrs. McCauley became sick, and Rosa left school again to look after her mother.

Rosa missed school. She wanted to get her high school diploma and make something of herself. But family responsibilities came first. Rosa's job was to look after her mother and the house. Sylvester worked as a carpenter and supported the family.

In 1931, Rosa met Raymond Parks. He was a gentle, hard-working barber in Montgomery. They dated for two years and were married in December 1932. Rosa was almost twenty years old, and Raymond was ten years older.

Parks, as Rosa called her husband, was a fine person in many ways. He encouraged his young wife to finish school. And at home he added to her education by sharing his knowledge and experience. Long before most people heard of civil rights, Raymond Parks was involved in the struggle for equality. He was a member of the NAACP and was glad when his wife wanted to join the group.

Times were hard for most Americans during the 1930s, especially for black people. Those were the years of the Great Depression. Millions of people were out of work. Rosa and Raymond Parks were lucky. Both of them had jobs. They didn't earn much, but they made enough with his barbering and her sewing to pay their bills.

At the end of 1941, the United States entered World War Two. Blacks and whites were drafted into the Army to fight for their country. But blacks weren't treated equally. Bigots and racists everywhere felt that liberty and justice were the rights of white people only.

Rosa Parks looked at the segregation all around her. She saw clearly that there was no liberty or justice for black people. She saw that there was a war to be fought at home: a peaceful war against injustice. For that reason she became very active in the NAACP.

Rosa Parks led a busy life. During the day, she worked at the Montgomery Fair Department Store. She also earned money doing sewing at home, and as a life-insurance agent.

Mrs. Parks's evenings and weekends were often spent working as the secretary of the local NAACP chapter. She kept a record of membership dues. She wrote letters and information bulletins that were sent around the country to newspapers, radio stations, NAACP contributors, and members.

Rosa Parks made sure that instances of discrimination and violence against blacks were recorded. She kept track of legal cases, jailings, lynchings, and other anti-black activities. All of this helped prepare her for her own place in black history. Then came that fateful day in December 1955, and Rosa Parks led the civil rights movement into a new era.

The bus boycott that followed Rosa Parks's brave deed lasted just over a year. On November 13, 1956, the Supreme Court declared the Montgomery bus segregation laws unconstitutional, and on December 20 the written order from the Supreme Court was received in Montgomery. The next day black people and white people rode the buses together, sitting wherever a seat was available.

The peaceful Montgomery bus boycott set an example that was followed throughout the South. Stores, lunch counters, bus stations, drinking fountains, rest rooms, hospitals...one by one, they became equally available to people of all races.

These victories didn't come easily. Churches were bombed, civil rights workers—black and white—were beaten and murdered. Rosa Parks lost her job at the department store and was unable to find work in Alabama. She and her family were threatened regularly. Raymond Parks also was unable to find work, and Mrs. McCauley was ill. Finally, in August 1957, the family left Alabama and moved to Detroit, Michigan. Sylvester McCauley, who had moved there years before, found an apartment for them to live in.

Rosa Parks stayed active in the civil rights movement. She also worked as an assistant to Representative John Conyers of Michigan. Congressman Conyers relied on Mrs. Parks to run his Detroit office while he was away in Washington, D.C. She remained in that job from 1965 through 1988.

At the age of seventy-five Mrs. Parks retired from her government job. But that wasn't the end of her life of service. In 1987, she founded The Rosa and Raymond Parks Institute for Self-Development. The goal of the institute is to provide education and guidance for young people. Mrs. Parks never forgot the sense of self-worth that molded her life. She wanted to pass on that quality to as many others as possible.

Many honors and words of praise were bestowed upon Rosa Parks. She was the mother of the civil rights movement, and words cannot do full justice to her accomplishments. But in Montgomery, Alabama, there is a special kind of monument that pleased Mrs. Parks very much. The bus on which she made history ran along Cleveland Avenue. Today, that street is called Rosa Parks Boulevard.

INDEX